FORD
CLASSICS

FORD
CLASSICS

BY THE AUTO EDITORS OF CONSUMER GUIDE®

Publications International, Ltd.

Louis Weber, CEO
Publications International, Ltd.
7373 North Cicero Avenue
Lincolnwood, Illinois 60712

Permission is never granted for commercial purposes.

ISBN-13: 978-1-4127-1525-6
ISBN-10: 1-4127-1525-3

Manufactured in China.

8 7 6 5 4 3 2 1

Library of Congress Control Number: 2007933679

Credits

Photography:
The editors would like to thank the following people and organizations for supplying the photography that made this book possible. They are listed below, along with the page number(s) of their photos.

Les Bidrawn: 15; **Thomas Glatch:** 33, 47, 65; **Sam Griffith:** 51; **Jerry Heasley:** 61; **Don Heiny:** 81, 93, 103; **Bud Juneau:** 9, 113; **Nick Komic:** 121; **Dan Lyons:** 37, 49; **Vince Manocchi:** 13, 19, 25, 31, 35, 39, 53, 57, 59, 73, 87, 91, 95, 128; **Doug Mitchel:** 21, 27, 29, 55, 77, 83, 99, 107, 115; **Mike Mueller:** 69; **David Newhardt:** 97, 109, 119; **Bob Nicholson:** 125; **Steve Statham:** 79; **Tom Strongman:** 11; **David Temple:** 63, 75, 101; **W.C. Waymack:** 17, 23, 41, 45, 67, 71, 85, 89, 105, 111, 117, 123; **Nicky Wright:** 43, 127

Back Cover: Les Bidrawn; Vince Manocchi; Doug Mitchel

Special thanks to: Kenneth F. Ruddock/Ken's Memory Lane

Owners:
Special thanks to the owners of the cars featured in this book for their cooperation. Their names and the page number(s) for their vehicles follow.

George Ball: 41; **Art Bancucci:** 9; **Paul Batista:** 57; **Gary Blakeslee:** 55; **Jack Buchanan:** 43; **Bob and Brad Chandler:** 69; **Edward and Arlene Cobb:** 49; **Dick Colarossi:** 31; **Keith Devereux:** 91; **Al DiSanti:** 11; **Tony Donna:** 39; **Ralph T. Dowling:** 81; **David Doyle:** 47; **Jeffrey M. Drucker:** 87; **Glenn Eisenhamer:** 99; **Fred C. Fischer:** 33; **Glen Gangestad:** 51; **Jack and Jan Garris:** 123; **Jerry Gibino:** 113; **Jerry and Alexandria Gundersen:** 29; **Buzz Gunnarson:** 13, 128; **Shel Harriman:** 19, back cover; **James Harris:** 101; **Lee Keeney:** 89; **James Kwiatkowski:** 107, back cover; **Douglas Leicht:** 27; **Tom Lerdahl:** 65; **Robert Lovato:** 53; **The W.M. Lyon Collection:** 25; **Larry Martin:** 71; **Russel L. Martin:** 121; **Bob Mayer:** 77; **Amos Minter:** 61; **Thomas G. Moore:** 109; **Gregg Cly's Mustang Muscle & More:** 79; **Dann Nixon:** 127; **Z.T. Parker:** 63; **Donald Passardi:** 37; **Joseph A. Pessetti:** 83; **Bob Peterson:** 125; **John Prokop:** 119; **Glen and Janice Pykiet:** 67; **Dorothy Quevreaux:** 105; **Robert Reeves:** 35, back cover; **Carl M. Riggins:** 15, back cover; **Donald and Marlene Schmidt:** 23; **Robert J. Secondi:** 115; **Sandra Simpkin:** 59, back cover; **Daniel P. Smith:** 21; **Sherm Smith:** 45; **Mike Spaziano:** 73; **Allan St. Jacques:** 97; **Seth Swoboda:** 17; **George and Gina Timm:** 111; **Martin J. Vehstedt:** 93; **Larry and Beverly Wake:** 85; **John and Connie Waugh:** 95; **Larry Webb:** 117; **Durwood Winchell:** 103; **Maurice Wright:** 75

CONTENTS

THERE'S A *Ford* IN YOUR FUTURE

FOREWORD

At the time of its founding in 1903, Ford Motor Company was merely one of dozens of upstart "horseless carriage" manufacturers vying for a foothold in a fledgling business. With continuous innovation and quality products, Ford quickly outpaced its rivals to become an industry-leading juggernaut that brought the era of the mass-produced automobile into existence. As the company flourished, its advertising progressed along with it. Over the years, workmanlike black-and-white renderings gave way to lavish full-color illustrations and sophisticated photography. Viewed from a historical perspective, each vintage ad is a wonderful time capsule of its era—from the heyday of the "Tin Lizzie" Model Ts to the chrome-bedecked, tailfinned dreamboats of the 1950s to the striped-and-spoiled muscle cars of the late 1960s and early '70s. Ford Classics pairs these evocative ads with beautiful contemporary photography that shows off pristine examples in impressive detail. Enjoy the highlights of this legendary automaker's vibrant and illustrious history.

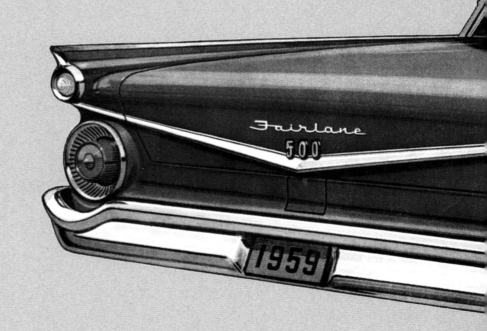

1911
MODEL T

Expanded manufacturing capacity enabled Ford
to offer considerable price cuts on all models for
1911. Touring cars like this one now started at
$780, or $170 less than the year before. Not surprisingly, sales improved. Factory output of touring
cars jumped to 26,405 for the fiscal year. In the ad
at left, Ford boasted about the Model T's economy
(20–28 miles per gallon), power-to-weight ratio (60
pounds per horsepower), and ample equipment
(two 6-inch gas lamps, three oil lamps, speedom-
eter, horn, and tools were standard on all models
shown). The ad also claimed that Model Ts could
get 5000 to 8000 miles on a single set of tires.

AS COOL in summer, as it is snug and weatherproof in winter, the Ford Closed Car has an unfailing appeal to women and children, who appreciate its many features of comfort.

Furnishings and equipment of the Sedan are of the highest order, including soft, durable cushions, revolving type window lifts, windshield visor, cowl ventilator, rugs, dome light, door locks, electric starting and lighting equipment.

And the Ford Closed Car costs so little to own and operate that mother and children can use it daily for every errand of business or pleasure.

TUDOR SEDAN, $590   FORDOR SEDAN, $685   COUPE, $525   (All prices f. o. b. Detroit)

CLOSED CARS

1924
MODEL T

The 10-millionth Model T rolled off the assembly line in June 1924. Prices dropped to new lows. Open-air models such as the runabout and touring car started at just $265 and $295, respectively. Closed cars like those shown here were pricier— $590 for a Tudor sedan or $685 for a Fordor sedan. The marketing of the increasingly affordable Model T attempted to position the vehicle not as a luxury, but as part of a normal middle-class lifestyle. While most automotive advertising targeted wealthy males, Ford pitched its cars as empowering for the common man, or woman. The company earned a record $100-million profit and held on to a 50-percent market share, though overall sales slipped slightly.

1926
MODEL T

The runabout body style continued as Ford's most-affordable model for 1926, with a starting price of just $290. Extra-cost special equipment included front and rear bumpers ($15), windshield wings ($6.50 a pair), top boot ($5), rearview mirror (75 cents), and wire wheels ($50 for a set of five, which dropped to $35 in late 1926). Wooden-spoked wheels were standard. The Model T's 176.7-cubic-inch four-cylinder made a mere 20 hp. Electric starters were newly standard on all Model T cars this year. Ford's market share fell to 36 percent as rival automakers ate away at the aging Model T's sales with fresher, more up-to-date competitive designs. The last Model T rolled off the line on May 26, 1927.

Spring brings beautiful colors for the new Ford car

MATCHING the fresh brilliance of Spring itself are the beautiful colors of the new Ford. They are rich in tone, yet carefully chosen, with a quiet good taste that endures.

There are eleven different Ford body types and all, with the single exception of the Station Wagon, are finished in a changing variety of colors.

You have the privilege of selecting from among these the color harmony that best suits your motoring needs and personal preference. Such choice is of course unusual in a low-price car and is one of the very special features of the new Ford.

Interior finish, upholstery and appointments are in keeping with this beauty of color and the trim, substantial lines which are so characteristically Ford. To the last least little detail, you can see evidence of the sincere quality that has been built into the car and the care that has been taken in its manufacture.

In all that goes to make a good automobile—in appearance—in safety—in comfort—in reliability—in economy—in alert satisfying performance—the new Ford is an unusual value at a low price. Its ease-of-operation and control and its freedom from mechanical troubles make it a particularly good car for a woman to drive.

Ford

FORD MOTOR COMPANY
Detroit, Michigan

1928
MODEL A

The long-awaited Model A was introduced to the public on December 2, 1927. A reported 10 million people came to see the revolutionary new Ford during its first 36 hours on the market. With a starting price of $585, the elegant Fordor sedan occupied the upper end of the price scale. The more-affordable roadster could be had with or without a rumble seat for the same price: $480. Handles and fender-mounted step plates aided rumble seat ingress and egress, but it was still a tricky process. This roadster is equipped with the optional trunk, radiator stone guard, and spare-tire cover. All Model As were powered by a new 200-cubic-inch four-cylinder that made 40 horsepower.

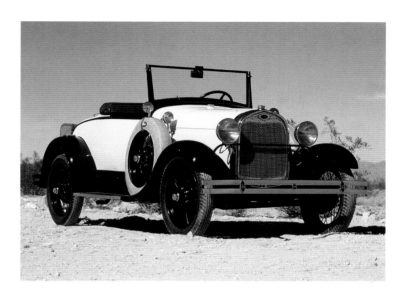

1931
MODEL A

Nineteen thirty-one was the last year of Model A production. Subtle styling changes included body-color sections in grille shelles and one-piece running board aprons. Sedan models and the Cabriolet were updated with slightly canted windshields late in the model year. The handsome Victoria body style was a mid-1930 addition to the Ford lineup. For the 1931 model year, it saw healthy sales of 33,906. The "Vicky" could be equipped with a rear-window sunshade and offered marginal luggage space behind the flip-down rear seatback. Despite a worsening Depression that caused Model A sales to tumble by more than 550,000 cars for the model year, the milestone 20-millionth Ford rolled off the assembly line on April 14, 1931.

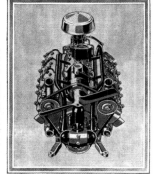

1932
MODEL 18

Fords were redesigned for 1932 with a longer wheelbase and handsome Lincoln-inspired design cues, but the real bombshell came on March 31, 1932, when Ford unveiled the first V-8 engine in the low-price field. The 221-cubic-inch "flathead" produced an advertised 65 horsepower. It leap-frogged the competition's six-cylinder engines and helped make the "Deuce" a holy grail among hot rodders. New styling touches like a vee'd body-color grille shell and ribbed single-bar bumpers bestowed a degree of elegance on '32 Fords. The five-passenger Victoria "coupe" was a particularly handsome body style that made the jump from the Model A era into the V-8 generation. It started at $550 with four-cylinder power, or $600 with the V-8.

THE
FORD
V·8

ONE ECONOMY YOU WILL ENJOY

WITH all its power, the Ford V-8 is a most economical car. Its V-8 cylinder engine actually uses no more fuel than a "four." It is saving of oil and tires. And the depreciation is probably less than you would expect. . . . To drive the Ford V-8 is thrift indeed. But it is also a most satisfying pleasure. Its superb performance is easy and sure. It shortens distances, not so much by reason of its potential top speed, but by the swiftness with which it resumes running speed after the inevitable stops and pauses. . . . We would like to have you know this car by driving it on the open road. Will you? Any Ford dealer will gladly put one in your hands.

1934
DeLUXE

After a complete redesign on a new, longer chassis for 1933, Ford cars saw only minor trim changes for 1934. By now, the Ford "flathead" V-8 was dominant; production of the Ford four-cylinder engine was discontinued in March 1934. To assuage potential buyers' concerns about fuel efficiency, the company comissioned "economy runs" in 1933 that showed results of 18.3 to 22.5 mpg in varied driving. Ford V-8 advertising touted economy as well as power. All regular-production '34 Ford cars wore rear-hinged "suicide" doors, which would soon become a thing of the past at Ford. The $570 V-8 DeLuxe five-window coupe's windshield could be cranked open and its rear window rolled down for interior ventilation.

FORD V·8

The Universal Car

ONE name comes quickly to mind when you think of "The Universal Car." The description is distinctively Ford. No other car is used by so many millions of men and women in every part of the world. Everywhere it is the symbol of faithful service. . . . That has always been a Ford fundamental. Something new is constantly being added in the way of extra value. Each year the Ford has widened its appeal by increasing its usefulness to motorists. . . . Today's Ford V-8 is more than ever "The Universal Car" because it encircles the needs of more people than any other Ford ever built. It reaches out and up into new fields because it has everything you need in a modern automobile. . . . The Ford V-8 combines fine-car performance, comfort, safety, beauty and convenience with low first cost and low cost of operation and up-keep. There is no other car like it in quality and price.

1935
DeLUXE

Sensational new looks, improved ride, and important mechanical improvements made the Model 48 Ford the best-selling car in America in 1935. Highlights of the new Ford look included a narrower, streamlined grille, sleek body-color "bullet" headlight shells, chrome-trimmed horizontal hood louvers, and enveloping fenders. External horns made their final appearance in '35. Buyers of DeLuxe Tudor and Fordor sedans could, for the first time, choose between the traditional "flatback" model or a new "trunkback" style. The DeLuxe Tudor Sedan (shown here), with its $575 base price, attracted 84,692 orders; the companion touring sedan with trunk started at $20 more and saw 87,326 copies.

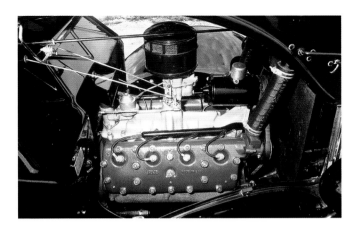

THE NEW FOUR-PASSENGER CLUB CABRIOLET

"Watch The Fords Go By"

Most often "it's a Ford" that steps out ahead at the traffic light. And does it so easily! No fuss or effort. Seems to just glide away in a smooth-flowing surge of power. . . . There's no surprise at this alert acceleration—you've come to expect it of a V-8. For many months, motorists have seen the Ford set the pace in traffic, on hills and on the open road. Frequently, you have heard it said—"The V-8 engine is the finest engine Ford has ever built." . . . Today's Ford gives you modern V-8 performance, with outstanding reliability and low cost. Its economy has been proved on the road by nearly three million Ford V-8 owners. . . . Each year the Ford brings you more in value—each year it costs less to run.

THE FORD V·8

$25 A MONTH, WITH USUAL DOWN-PAYMENT, BUYS ANY NEW FORD V-8 CAR ON NEW UCC ½ PER CENT PER MONTH FINANCE PLANS

1936
DeLUXE

For 1936, Fords received a handsome facelift that included graceful V-shaped grille with vertical bars. Horns were now hidden behind front-fender-mounted grilles. Wire spokes were replaced across the line by new "artillery-style" wheels. The sole powerplant remained the 221-cubic-inch, 85-horsepower "flathead." The V-8 engine was still a competitive advantage, but Henry Ford stubbornly refused to add modern features such as all-steel "turret" tops, hydraulic brakes, and independent front suspension, despite these features appearing on competitors' models. Shown here is the rakish-looking DeLuxe cabriolet, which started at $625 and attracted 14,068 orders.

"Don't worry, lady—we *couldn't* make the road rough enough to be risky for a Ford!"

BYWAYS ARE HIGHWAYS IN THE NEW FORD V·8

Ford V·8

FOR 1937

THE famous old Ford Model T actually <u>made</u> roads where none existed. And today's handsome Ford V-8 has the same rugged dependability built into every inch of it.

Confidence makes cross-country miles more <u>fun</u> in a Ford. You <u>know</u> you have plenty of responsive power for any situation. You <u>know</u> you'll ride safely and comfortably. So you drive relaxed and arrive rested.

Many factors contribute to Ford comfort. . . . The Center-Poise principle, by which passengers are cradled

near the <u>center</u> of the car and even the back seat is seven inches ahead of the rear axle. . . . High steering ratio. . . . Low center of gravity. . . . Flexible springs and <u>adjustable</u> shock absorbers. . . . Wide seats. . . . And the <u>extra</u> body room made possible by a compact V-type 8-cylinder engine.

With a <u>choice</u> of two sizes of this modern power plant — with new operating economy, the lowest price in years and distinctive features all around—the 1937 Ford V-8 is very definitely THE QUALITY CAR IN THE LOW-PRICE FIELD.

Ford

1937
DELUXE

As per the industry trend, Fords became more streamlined for 1937. Headlamps were incorporated into the front fender aprons, and the prominently vee'd grille was stretched and sloped back. Fenders were curvier. A smaller-displacement version of Ford's existing 85-horsepower V-8, rated at 60 horsepower, was introduced. The "V-8/60," available on all but DeLuxe models, was aimed at buyers looking for a standard-size car that was cheaper to operate than a larger eight. The pitch had merit, but Americans found the engine underpowered. The "trunkback" DeLuxe Tudor and Fordor sedans (shown here) handily outsold their "slantback" counterparts.

"Oh, Darling! It's so lovely that I haven't a thing to go with it!"

We do hope your new Ford arrives by daylight!

Above: the De Luxe Ford V-8 Fordor Sedan in Dartmouth Green; 85 hp.

Below: the Ford V-8 Tudor Sedan in Gull Gray; 85 or 60 hp.

YOU'RE going to be a very proud lady . . . whether this is your first Ford or your tenth. It's the biggest beauty that ever rolled up to your door and set hearts and window-curtains stirring!

The lines of this new car are as long and smooth and graceful as a plume. The space inside is amazing! You'll want to lounge, luxuriously, in the redesigned seats which are deeper and softer, over the car's long flexible springs and hydraulic shock absorbers.

And the new quiet is something you can actually sense. Scientific soundproofing has made the Ford such a restful companion! As you travel together . . . in traffic lines or country lanes . . . there's the safety of an all-steel body and new hydraulic brakes. And the velvety V-8 engine makes driving as smooth as dreaming!

The 1939 Fords are modernly, modestly priced. And of this, you're always sure: Ford-built means top value . . . as well as top vogue. Ford Motor Company now offers Ford, Mercury, Lincoln-Zephyr and Lincoln motor cars.

FEATURES THAT MAKE FORD CARS TOP VALUE

★ **STYLE LEADERSHIP** — *The luxury car in the low-price field.*

★ **V-TYPE 8-CYLINDER ENGINE** — *8 cylinders give smoothness. Small cylinders give economy.*

★ **HYDRAULIC BRAKES**—*Easy-acting—quick, straight stops.*

★ **TRIPLE-CUSHIONED COMFORT**—*New flexible roll-edge seat cushions, soft transverse springs, hydraulic shock absorbers.*

★ **STABILIZED CHASSIS** — *No front end bobbing or dipping. Level starts, level stops, level ride.*

★ **SCIENTIFIC SOUNDPROOFING** — *Noises hushed for quiet ride.*

★ **LOW PRICES** — *Advertised prices include many items of desirable equipment.*

DE LUXE FORD V·8

1939
DeLUXE

DeLuxe Fords got new front end styling with a bright vertical bar grille and relocated headlights. A deep, enveloping "alligator" hood finally did away with separate side panels and made engine access easier. Standard models made do with mildly facelifted '38 sheetmetal. With 144,333 units produced, the DeLuxe Tudor Sedan was easily the best seller in the line. All Ford products finally adopted hydraulic brakes this year, well after they were commonplace among competitive makes. Henry Ford had stubbornly believed that hydraulic brakes were unsafe, and forbid their use in his company's vehicles, but eventually gave in to the urging of his corporate advisors.

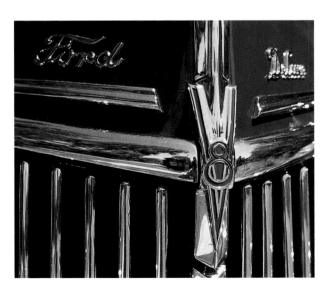

Modern Cars for Modern Highways

Watch the FORDS go by!

Through crowded city canyons . . . down busy small-town Main Streets . . . past pleasant country cross-roads . . . *the 1940 Fords are going by!*

Big cars, these — with long, low hoods and flowing lines. . . . *Colorful* cars — with lustrous, lasting enamel baked into the body metal and rustless steel shining bright. . . . *Comfortable* cars — with rich appointments, deep, soft seats and a quiet, restful ride.

 Ten years ago, you couldn't have bought cars so fine at *any* price —

and you would have paid several hundred dollars more for a smooth, sweet-running V-8 engine!

More than 27,000,000 Ford cars — far more than any other make — have gone out to serve the world. The experience gained in building nearly one-third of all the cars *ever* built contributes to the excellence of today's Ford cars.

The low-priced 1940 Ford V-8 has all the honest value Ford owners have come to expect plus many modern features that make it more than ever The Quality Car in the Low-price Field.

1940
DeLUXE

A subtle but handsome facelift marked 1940 Ford DeLuxe models. Styling highlights included sealed beam headlamps, a horizontal bar grille, and unique "chevron" taillights. A decidedly modern new dash featured a maroon-and-sand two-tone finish, rectangular instrument panel, and an ashtray on both sides. The DeLuxe convertible was up $60 to $849, but now boasted a hydraulically powered top. A rumble seat, however, was no longer available. Crank-out windshields were also a thing of the past, as front window ventipanes and a pop-up cowl vent now provided interior ventilation. This Mandarin Maroon convertible is equipped with the optional bumper guards, wheel trim rings, and heater.

There will always be *one* test we can't make

IN BUILDING THE FORD BUSINESS, we have not leaned primarily on salesmanship to make our cars successful with the public. Instead, we aim to build a product so outstanding in its value that it will largely sell itself to the buyer who knows real motor car quality.

To that end we design a car today that includes many features found at higher prices, but not found elsewhere at our price level.

Then, in building today's Ford, we test

the job we do with equipment that is more remarkable than any ever developed before.

Testing machines used in making Ford parts, for instance, hold accuracy at many points to ten-thousandths of an inch, and in some cases can measure down to millionths.

From the assembly line, at regular intervals, a car is sent to the Ford "torture track," to be sped, skidded, wrenched, jolted and shocked to test the very limits of its great endurance.

In the Ford weather tunnel still other tests go on in the face of man-made weather as severe as any to be found anywhere in the world.

Here in the big Rouge Plant, we satisfy ourselves as to the quality of our cars by the hardest tests that we know how to make.

The single test we can't make comes when you get behind the wheel and go. And because we know so well what that will show, we are more than glad to stand by its result!

Some Ford Advantages for 1941:

NEW ROOMINESS. Bodies are longer and wider this year, adding as much as seven inches to seating width.

SOFT, QUIET RIDE. A new Ford ride, with new frame and stabilizer, softer springs, improved shock absorbers.

POWER WITH ECONOMY. This year, more than ever, Ford owners are enthusiastic about the economy and fine all-round performance of Ford cars.

BIG WINDOWS. Windshield and windows increased all around to give nearly four square feet of added vision area in each '41 Ford Sedan.

LARGEST HYDRAULIC BRAKES in the Ford price field, give added safety, longer brake-lining wear.

GET THE FACTS AND YOU'LL GET A FORD!

1941
SUPER DeLUXE

Ford's new '41 models were bigger in most every dimension and sported a unique three-section grille. The model line expanded to include three trim levels: Special, DeLuxe, and Super DeLuxe. All could be had with the flathead V-8, which now produced 90 hp, or a new L-head six-cylinder engine that made 85. The convertible body style was exclusive to the Super DeLuxe series. The chrome windshield and fender trim on this convertible identify it as a late 1941 model. Inside, Super DeLuxe models got a glovebox-mounted clock, a steering wheel chrome trim ring, crank-controlled vent windows, plastic "Kelobra"-grain dash trim, and twin sunvisors.

FOR 1942

A Beautiful New FORD

6 or 8 cylinders

1942

IN THESE UNUSUAL TIMES we invite you to inspect an unusual new car—new in its beauty, its comfort, its choice of two fine 90 horsepower engines, 6 cylinders or 8.

See it and you sense at once that here is new style that will *stay* good for years. On a lower, wider chassis, we have designed new long, low, wide and modern lines.

Interior treatment is entirely fresh, distinctive, pleasing. The modern beauty of this Ford, seen from inside or out, will more than hold its own in any company.

Inside, the car is *big* in every way—wide across the seats, generous in knee-room, leg-room, elbow-room.

On the road this year you find the "new Ford ride" still further advanced in its softness, quietness, steadiness.

At the wheel, you will find driving easier than ever. Steering, gear-shifting, action of the big and sure hydraulic brakes have all been made smoother and easier.

In quality, the car is sound to the last detail. Defense require-

ments have all been met without a single reduction in the basic and lasting goodness of the Ford mechanically. Some new materials have replaced old ones, usually at greater cost to us, *but in every case the new is equal to or better than the old.*

If your family needs a new car, go see and drive this Ford. *For what it is today and for what it will be through the years ahead, we believe that you will find in it more and better transportation for your money than you have ever found before.*

Ford

1942
SUPER DeLUXE

The 1942 Fords were introduced on September 12, 1941, about three months before America entered World War II. Updates included a new front end with a rectangular grille, new oval-shaped taillights, and a symmetrical dash with round gauges. The Super DeLuxe station wagon remained the most-expensive Ford at $1115 with the flathead six or $1125 with the V-8. Ford subtly acknowledged the heightening global unrest with the opening line of this ad: "In these unusual times we invite you to inspect an unusual new car..." The model year was cut short as Detroit factories were repurposed to support the war effort. After months of increasing government restrictions on materiels usage, civilian car production ended on February 10, 1942.

NEW 1946 FORD SPORTSMAN'S CONVERTIBLE!

Outside and inside, there never was a car like this before!
The new Ford Sportsman's Convertible is really *two* cars in one!
Ford designers have combined the paneled smartness of the
station wagon and the touch-a-button convenience of the convertible!

Something really
NEW!

BIG NEW 100 H.P. V-8

makes Ford the liveliest performer
of all the low-priced cars!
New 4-ring aluminum pistons and
new balanced carburetion
make the big Ford V-8
thrifty on gas and oil!

JUST TOUCH A BUTTON

. . . and in 30 seconds you have a
snug "sedan" that's weather-tight!
With the top up or with it down, the
Sportsman's Convertible is a honey for looks!

IT TAKES A TRUNK

There's room galore in this new
luggage compartment . . . just as
there's room galore for six grown-ups
in the wide leather seats!

NEW OVERSIZED BRAKES

. . . self-centering and hydraulic . . . with
big 12-inch brake drums . . . to give you
smooth, straight-line stops on all
road surfaces. Quiet!
Easy-acting. Long-life linings!

THERE'S A *Ford* IN YOUR FUTURE

TUNE IN . . . The FORD-Bob Crosby Show — CBS, Wednesdays, 9:30-10 P.M., E.S.T. . . . The FORD Sunday Evening Hour — ABC, Sundays, 8-9 P.M., E.S.T.

1946
SPORTSMAN

The 1946 Fords were basically warmed-over 1942s but nonetheless boasted numerous improvements. Among them were a horizontal bar grille, a larger, 100-hp flathead V-8 lifted from the upscale Mercury line, and an upgraded interior. Eager shoppers, hungry for new cars after a four-year drought, snapped up the new models. A midyear addition to the line was the unusual Sportsman, a wood-sided convertible model that listed for a hefty $1982—a full $494 more than a regular ragtop. This, combined with the additional maintenance of the wood body components, limited sales to just 1209 units. Still, the Sportsman did inject some additional interest into what was essentially a prewar car line.

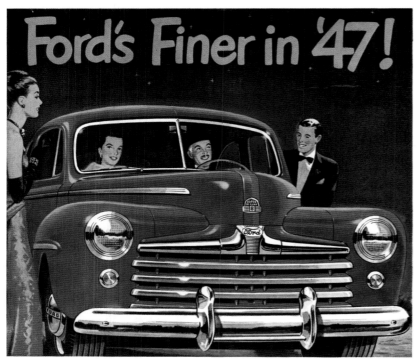

Ford's Finer in '47!

Spring's smartest styling...inside and out!

Any way you look at it, today's Ford is by far the smartest car in the low-priced field. One look and you know it's got style . . . from stem to stern . . . inside and out!

With all these new style features . . . A newly styled instrument panel with big new dials for easy reading . . . new body colors . . . new front-end appearance . . . new stainless steel body molding . . . new hood medallion . . . newly fashioned door handles . . . new wheel rims and hub caps . . . new heavier bumper guards—And many other new features!

Listen to the Ford Show starring Dinah Shore on Columbia Network stations Wed. evenings.

There's a FINER 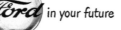 in your future

1947
SUPER DeLUXE

Fords saw only minor detail changes for 1947, such as relocated parking lights and revised interior trim. Woody wagons remained part of the lineup, all wearing Super DeLuxe trim. Priced at $1972 with a V-8 ($1893 with the six-cylinder engine), the four-door wagon held eight passengers. Middle- and third-row seats could be removed for added cargo space. A total of 16,104 were built, slightly fewer than in 1946. Though the product line didn't show it yet, this was the dawn of a new era at Ford Motor Company. Corporate patriarch Henry Ford died at the age of 83 on April 7, 1947, and his grandson Henry II was settling in to his new position as president.

Wool, and lots of it, goes into Ford upholstery. No wonder it wears so well and looks so beautiful.

V-8 or Six, there's horsepower to spare in the Ford.

No matter how much moola you lay on the line, Ford is the only car to offer you a choice of a V-8 or a Six!

Ford's out Front down on the Farm

There's nothing stubborn about the way Ford starts. Just touch a button and you take off!

You can run a Ford almost for chicken feed, thanks to 4-ring aluminum pistons and balanced carburetion. Ford economy is something to crow about!

A cat can look at a queen and that's what the Ford car is — a "queen" inside and out.

There's a *Ford* in your future

*No use Mac. You can't beat a Ford!"

Listen to the Ford Theater over NBC stations Sunday afternoon 5:00 to 6:00 P.M. E.S.T.

1948
SUPER DeLUXE

Despite the praise from these barnyard aficionados, there was nothing new about the 1948 Fords—they were basically straight carryovers from 1947. The Super DeLuxe sedan coupe model listed for $1409 and offered seating for six, though back seat space was cramped. Hood badges denoted whether the six or V-8 was underhood. Total Ford production hit around 248,000, down from 429,000 units for 1947. The drop in output was attributable to an abbreviated model year—production of the 1948 models was halted to make way for the all-new 1949 models, which debuted in June 1948.

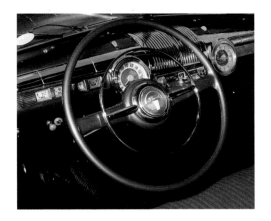

1949
CUSTOM

Ford's first redesigned postwar models debuted for the 1949 model year. They were new inside and out—underneath, transverse "buggy springs" were dropped in favor of independent front suspension and rear parallel leaf springs. Modern, slab-sided fenders were a clear departure from the bulbous fenders of previous years. A "propeller spinner" centered between horizontal grille bars highlighted front end styling. A "6" or "8" in the center of the grille spinner indicated the 226-cid inline flathead six or the 239-cid flathead V-8, both carryover engines. Naturally, the flashiest body style was the $1886 convertible, which attracted more than 51,000 customers.

1950
CUSTOM

After their revolutionary 1949 redesign, Fords received only minor updates for 1950. Most visible among them were a new Ford crest on the hood and decklid, a slightly revised grille with parking lamps located below the grille bar, and a new steering wheel horn ring. Functional changes included pushbutton door handles and a gas filler located behind a hinged flap. Overall quality was much improved over the hastily assembled '49s—bodies and frames were strengthened, handling upgraded, and the V-8 engine quieted. Custom Fordor sedans started at $1558, $47 more than a Custom club coupe. Whitewalls, trim rings, and ribbed fender skirts were extra-cost options.

1951
CUSTOM

A new "dual-spinner" grille was the most visible of the year's trim changes, and Ford's first automatic transmission, the three-speed Ford-O-Matic, debuted as a $164 option. Ads claimed it "cuts 92% of your driving motions!" Minor improvements to the 239-cid V-8 included a waterproof ignition system and a larger-capacity fuel pump, but output remained unchanged at 100 horsepower. The wood-sided Country Squire remained the sole station wagon and was also the priciest Ford at $2029. Its sales rose to 29,017 for the model year. All other 1951 Fords got a flashy new dashboard design, but the Squire made do with a wood-toned version of the previous year's panel.

NEWEST car under the sun!

Here's the '52 Ford Sunliner—Queen of the Convertibles! Touch a button and the top raises in seconds to give you the snugness of a closed car. Car illustrated is Alpine Blue with interior trim of blue leather and vinyl.

ABLEST car on the American road!

An eye-corner glance tells you that no car—not even one costing far more—has more perfect line and grace than a '52 Ford.

And then, close up, you find that every detail reveals the kind of skilled workmanship that only comes from expert hands.

But there's something else, and this you've got to feel: Ford "can do." It's what comes from the most powerful engine in its field—110 high-compression horsepower—V-8 style! It's the extra dividend of comfort assured by Ford's own

Automatic Ride Control . . . the easy passage over roughest roads, the level rounding of curves.

And it's the freedom from work, for Fordomatic takes over the shifting. You guide a Ford from an uncluttered cockpit as wide as a sofa. And "*guide*" is the word. .

That's Ford "can do". . . and for the fun of a real heart-warming experience, please "Test Drive" it today!

Fordomatic, white sidewall tires optional at extra cost. Equipment, accessories and trim subject to change without notice.

'52 FORD

you can pay more... but you can't buy better!

Here's the '52 Ford Victoria—America's best-dressed "hard top." Notice how side windows slide away.

1952
CRESTLINE

Ford cars got their second full restyle in three years for 1952. Round taillights, a one-piece windshield, and discreet rear fender bulges were visual highlights of the new body design, while a sturdy new "K-bar" frame helped improve overall rigidity. A redesigned interior featured a "Flight-Style Control Panel" and "Power Pivot" suspended pedals. The model lineup was revamped to include Mainline, Customline, and Crestline trim levels. Ford's first true hardtop model, the Victoria, debuted—this example wears 1953 horizontal chrome strips on its rear fenders. Underhood, the big news was a peppy new "Mileage Maker" six that put out 101 horses. To keep pace, the flathead V-8 received a 10-hp hop-up, boosting its output to 110 hp.

Again for '53...
FORD'S out Front
with the new STANDARD of the AMERICAN ROAD

The one V-8 in its field is the Ford V-8. You get top "Go" per gallon because its Automatic Power Pilot squeezes high-compression power from regular gas. You'll find this feature, too, in Ford's 101-h.p. Mileage Maker Six.

Power Pivot Pedals are suspended from above to work easier and eliminate drafty floor holes... to give you increased foot room. Only Ford, in its field, has them.

Center-Fill Fueling prevents hose marks from marring the finish of your car... eliminates gas spilling on fenders. It also makes filling up easy from either side of gas pump. And the shorter fill pipe gives more luggage space in trunk.

I-REST tinted safety glass makes driving easier on your eyes. Green tint cuts reflections, road glare.

Full-Circle Visibility with car-wide rear window... curved, one-piece windshield, big picture windows all around.

Fordomatic Drive, Overdrive, I-REST tinted glass, white sidewall tires optional at extra cost. Equipment, accessories and trim subject to change without notice.

And with 41 "Worth More" features, it's worth more when you buy it ... worth more when you sell it!

Hull-Tight Construction and K-Bar reinforced box section frame give Ford top strength for weight. You ride in dust-free, draft-free comfort in a car that's designed to stay "tight" for years to come. And this Ford will keep looking young for many seasons, thanks to Ford's baked enamel finish.

Shift to Fordomatic and you'll never shift again. It's the finest, most versatile of the Automatic drives. And remember only Ford in its field lets you choose between Fordomatic, Overdrive or Conventional Drive.

New Miracle Ride... NOTHING EVER LIKE IT! NOT JUST NEW, MORE RESPONSIVE SPRINGS AND "SHOCKS," NOT JUST FOAM-RUBBER CUSHIONS. HERE IS A COMPLETELY BALANCED RIDE THAT GIVES YOU AN ENTIRELY NEW CONCEPT OF COMFORT.

Counterbalancing Space Saver Hinges lift the deck lid when you turn the key. Space Saver hinge design also helps give Ford the most trunk space in its field. The hood, too, is counterbalanced to open automatically and stay open till it's closed.

Never before in history were the demands on a car so great! You "live" more in your car... so you need more living room (and luggage space), so you drive greater distances, so you need a car with lots of "Go," yet one that's light on gas.

Good roads are better, bad roads are worse. So you want riding qualities that set an entirely new standard of smoothness on all roads... plus almost effortless steering, braking and parking.

And, of course, you want the style-setter... a car that belongs wherever you may drive.

ONLY FORD GIVES YOU SO MANY THINGS YOU NEED AND WANT FOR SO LITTLE MONEY.

See the big '53 Ford. Value Check its 41 "Worth More" features. Test Drive the '53 Ford. You'll agree that here is the New Standard of the American Road!

wow!

No wonder the swing is to FORD!

1953
CRESTLINE

Ford Motor Company celebrated its 50th anniversary in 1953 with an attractively facelifted car. Styling revisions included a new grille with a "bullet" hub and a ribbed crossbar, rectangular parking lights, and twin-section taillights. Steering wheels got a special 50th anniversary commemorative medallion. Advertising pushed resale value and boasted 41 "Worth More" features such as "Magic Action" double-sealed brakes, "Presto-Lift" counterbalanced hood, and "I-REST" tinted safety glass. Most glamorous of the offerings was the Crestline Sunliner convertible, which cost $2043 with standard V-8. A specially decorated Sunliner was the official pace car of the 1953 Indianapolis 500.

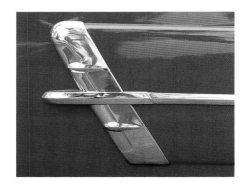

Only Y-block V-8 engine in its field—with low-friction design and turbo-wedge combustion chambers for the most advanced V-8 power in the industry.

Only Ball-Joint Front Suspension in its field—with weight-tailored, Hydra-Coil Front Springs for a far smoother ride on all roads.

Only car in its field with so many Trend-Setting advances—such as Center-Fill Fueling, suspended clutch and brake pedals and signal lights for oil and generator.

Only Hulltight Body in its field—with sound-insulation under the roof, floor and hood . . . and all around . . . for much greater comfort and quiet.

Only car in its field with so many features that are found in costliest cars—such as full Hotchkiss drive, riveted brake lining and glass-fibre hood insulation.

Only car in its field with such high resale value. Analysis of used car prices shows that Ford cars return more of their original cost on resale than any competitive car.

—and you'll

Your Ford Dealer invites you to take a Test Drive

1954
MAINLINE

Fords again wore minor trim changes for 1954 but got some significant engineering improvements. The long-lived flathead V-8 was retired in favor of an all-new overhead-valve V-8. Dubbed "Y-Block" because of its cross-sectional shape, the new engine displaced the same 239.4 cubic inches as its L-head predecessor but produced 20 more horse-power—130 to the old flathead's 110. Underneath, a more-sophisticated ball-joint front suspension replaced the previous kingpin setup. At $1898, the Crestline four-door sedan (left) was the most-affordable member of the line-topping Crestline series. The no-frills Mainline (right) started at $1701. This one is equipped with the optional Y-Block, which added about $80 to the base price.

New **FAIRLANE** series. The luxurious new 4-door Fairlane Town Sedan (illustrated above) is but one of the six distinguished models in this all-new line, which also includes two new Crown Victorias . . . new Sunliner . . . new Victoria . . . new 2-door Club Sedan.

New **MAINLINE** series. A new Business Sedan joins the Fordor (illustrated) and Tudor models. As in all '55 Fords, there are new larger brakes . . . new tubeless tires.

'55 Ford

WORTH MORE WHEN YOU BUY IT...
WORTH MORE WHEN YOU SELL IT!

1955
SUNLINER

Fords got dramatic new sheetmetal for 1955, highlighted by peaked headlight bezels, a wraparound windshield, small tailfins, and "Jet-Tube" taillights. Flashy "checkmark" bodyside trim identified the new Fairlane series, which replaced Crestline as the poshest Ford. The new trim lent itself to attractive two-tone paint combinations, such as the Tropical Rose and Snowshoe White combo on this Sunliner convertible. Midlevel Customline models wore more-subdued chrome trim, while the entry-level Mainline models had no side trim. Ford's "Y-Block" V-8 was enlarged to 272 cubic inches and made 162 horsepower, or 182 hp with the "Power-Pack" four-barrel carburetor/dual exhaust option.

The Thunderbird is now available in 5 colors!

6 a.m. THUNDERBIRD time

Doctor, Lawyer, Merchant, Chief—no matter who you are—you'll find yourself getting up early when your garage is home to a Thunderbird. For here is a truly delightful package of sheer pleasure—all the way from its "let's go" look to the "let's go" performance of its Thunderbird Special Y-block V-8.

What's more—that comfortable seat is nearly *five* feet wide and it's power-operated. The steering wheel is still another comfort feature

—adjust it in or out, as *you* like it.

As for weather—your Thunderbird can have an easily demountable hard top *and/or* a snug fabric top. Windows roll up . . . power-operated if you like. Power steering, power brakes, Overdrive and Speed-Trigger Fordomatic are also available. These are important details, but the main thing is the low and mighty car itself! Why don't you obey that urge and try one today. Your Ford Dealer is the man to see.

This is the Thunderbird Special Y-block V-8 4-barrel carburetor, 8.5 to 1 compression ratio, 198-h.p. with Fordomatic . . . try it!

An exciting original by **FORD**

1955
THUNDERBIRD

Ford answered Chevrolet's Corvette with a two-seater of its own, the dazzling 1955 Thunderbird. Ford's stylish "personal car" was instantly popular and a great image builder for the company. A standard 292-cid V-8 from the Mercury line produced 193 horsepower when equipped with the three-speed manual transmission, or 198 hp with Ford-O-Matic. As seen here, Ford offered a removable hardtop in addition to the typical retractable soft top. Styling details included a functional hood scoop, tasteful chrome trim accents, and rear bumper "bombs" that contained the exhaust outlets. Unlike Corvette, with its drafty side curtains, the T-Bird included roll-up windows and a selection of power extras, all aimed at luxury-minded buyers.

The new Victoria . . . one of Ford's 18 models for '56

You'll be safer in a '56 Ford !

For 1956, Ford announces the first major contribution to passenger and driver protection in accidents: New Lifeguard Design! It is the end result of more than two years of research by Ford in co-operation with universities, medical associations, and safety experts. It is designed to give you added protection in the areas where *the majority of serious accident injuries occur.*

You get this Lifeguard protection in a car unmatched for beauty . . . with styling inspired by the Ford Thunderbird. What's more, Ford brings you the sheer delight of commanding the new 202-h.p. Thunderbird Y-8 engine* — a new smooth-running, Go-packed, deep-block engine that will put fresh enthusiasm into all your driving.

*In Fordomatic Fairlane and Station Wagon models

New Lifeguard steering wheel

Safety experts called for a wheel that would protect the driver from the steering post in an accident. The deep-center structure of Ford's new Lifeguard steering wheel provides a cushioning effect under impact.

New Lifeguard door latches

Safety experts say that passengers are considerably safer in accidents if they stay inside the car. Ford's new Lifeguard double-grip door locks reduce the possibility of doors springing open under strain and occupants being thrown from the car.

New Ford seat belts

Safety experts asked for belts to hold driver and passengers securely in their seats in sudden stops. Ford's optional nylon-rayon cord seat belts are solidly anchored to the steel flooring and will withstand a force of 4,000 lbs.!

New Lifeguard padding

Safety experts recommend cushioning hard surfaces within a car to reduce head injuries. Ford's optional Lifeguard padding on control panel and sun visors absorbs impacts . . . helps to guard you from injury.

1956
CROWN VICTORIA

A smart, subtle facelift graced 1956 Fords with a wide-grate grille and horizontal parking lights in wraparound chrome pods. Under general manager Robert S. McNamara, Ford engineers conducted extensive factory crash testing in 1955. This research resulted in several "Lifeguard Design" features for '56. The flagship Crown Victoria entered its second and final season as Ford's glitter king. Of the 9812 Crown Vics built for '56, just 603 were Skyliners. The Skyliner's tinted Plexiglass roof panel was a novel idea that drew traffic on the showroom floor, but its high cost and sweltering cabin temperatures on sunny days limited sales. This example is equipped with Ford's top engine choice for the year, a 225-hp, 312-cid V-8.

Hard top, soft top or open—the Thunderbird is the star in *any* setting!

And now: the latest version

of America's most exciting car:

Ford THUNDERBIRD for '56

Ready to give you a new lease on driving fun, this newest version of America's favorite dream car is more stunning in style . . . more thrilling in power . . . more luxurious in comfort.

Here, poised for flight you see what many people hardly dreamed possible: a more beautiful, more powerful, more distinctive Thunderbird.

The graceful contours of its long, low lines . . . the unique flair of its new spare-tire mounting . . . the dazzling sheen of its new two-tone colors are but a hint of its newness.

It is when you put the selector in drive position and nudge the gas pedal of a Fordomatic model

that the new Thunderbird will really take you by the heart. Nestled beneath that sleek hood lies a new 225-h.p. Thunderbird Y-8, ready to revise all your ideas of how a car should respond.

Now, you may choose hard top, soft top or both. There's a glass-fibre hard top and a foldaway fabric top. Now, the interiors are richer—more beautiful than ever. Now, you get the added protection of Ford's exclusive Lifeguard design. Now, the ride is smoother—the cornering is flatter than ever. And, as always, you may have optional power steering, brakes, windows and seat. Ask your Ford Dealer just how soon *you* can start enjoying the better things of driving.

The 1956 Thunderbird's brand-new rear spare-tire mounting folds back handily, as quick as a wink. It adds as greatly to your luggage space as it does to the over-all beauty of the car.

1956
THUNDERBIRD

Thunderbirds got a handful of minor updates for '56, including sunvisors, glass wind wings, dashboard padding, and a deep-dish steering wheel. Thunderbird badges on the hood and trunklid replaced checkered-flag emblems. New flip-open vents on the front fenders funneled fresh air into the cockpit, and the standard continental spare tire improved trunk space and weight distribution. Addressing complaints of poor over-the-shoulder visibility, porthole windows were now available on the optional hardtop; buyers chose it four-to-one over the blind-quarter version. Weight and price crept up to 3038 pounds and $3151, and sales dropped to 15,631 units. Wide whitewalls and wire wheel covers remained popular options.

Announcing ⬡ *for '57*

a new kind of FORD

with the touch of tomorrow... and Thunderbird go

After today, American cars will never be the same again... for the Big New Kind of Ford is a brilliant new automotive package—the only <u>fine car</u> in the low-price field!

■ You're looking at a new adventure named Ford! Ever see a car so low? It's just shoulder high, yet it's easier to enter and roomier than ever. And ever see such a long car in Ford's field? It looks as long as a yacht and twice as lovely.

But your real thrill comes when this Ford shows its stuff! The new Silver Anniversary V-8's, up to 245 hp strong, make driving easier than ever. And for super

economy, try a new Mileage Maker Six.

It handles as if it reads your mind. It corners on the level. It takes the bounce out of bumps with its deep-cradle ride. It laughs off the miles. It's quiet as a mouse in sneakers. And, the completely new Inner Ford has the built-in extra quality to *keep* that wonderful new-car feel. Best of all, you get all this at low Ford prices. *See the new kind of Ford today!*

You'll sit sweet, low and pretty, inside the new built-for-keeps body

For Ford brings you the most comfortable, most luxurious, most completely insulated body ever in the low-price field. How do you like these new fabrics and that new panel—with all controls recessed?

'57
FORD
prestige car of the low price field

The only low-priced car that comes in two sizes

The Custom and Custom 300
are over 16 feet long

All 5 models in the Custom and Custom 300 series ride on a big new 116-inch wheelbase—longest in the low-price field. And Ford's five beautiful *new* station wagons all ride on their own special chassis, too. They are longer, lower, heavier, with more room, more look-out area, the smoothest, quietest station wagon ride ever.

The Fairlane and Fairlane 500
are over 17 feet long

Meet the '57 cars that make *big* a low-priced word! Whether you choose a new Fairlane (4 models) or Fairlane 500 (5 models), you get a car over 9 inches longer, as much as 4 inches lower. They ride on a big 118-inch wheelbase. And, thanks to the new slim chrome body pillars, even *sedans* have that "hardtop" look!

1957
FAIRLANE 500

For 1957, Fords were new from the ground up and longer, lower, and wider than before. Bodies were bigger and bolder, with "sculptured" shapes and more-prominent tailfins. The model lineup was revamped to comprise Custom and Custom 300 models on a 116-inch wheelbase and Fairlane and Fairlane 500 models on a 118-inch wheelbase. Flashy two-tone paint was available on all. Engine choices ranged from 144-hp, 223-cid "Mileage Maker" six to a "Thunderbird 312" V-8 that put out 245 horsepower with a single four-barrel carburetor, or 270 with dual quads. Fairlane and Fairlane 500 sedans had a hardtop look thanks to their thin, chrome-plated door pillars, as seen on this Fairlane 500 club sedan.

YIPPEE

– it's more than a car!
– it's more than a truck!

It's the brand-new FORD RANCHERO

A cargo-carrying work horse! Actually packs more payload than many standard pickups. Power to spare, too—modern Short Stroke 144 hp Six or either of two Short Stroke V-8s: 192 hp in the Ranchero and 212 hp in the Custom Ranchero. Fordomatic or Overdrive available.

A smooth-handling show pony! Ball-joint front suspension and outboard-mounted rear springs—first time on any pickup—give true car ride. Cab interior is exactly like that of a '57 Ford Ranch Wagon. Power steering, power brakes, power seat and power windows available.

Any way you look at it, the stunning new Ranchero is the slickest, sleekest Pickup ever to pack a load.

And what a load! The Ranchero carries over half a ton—more than many standard pickups! The body floor is over six feet long, and has a lower loading height than any other pickup. It's as handy as it is husky!

And when work is done, this pack horse turns into a fun-loving show pony! It gives you all the luxury and handling ease of a fine car, just right for those trips to town, for after-work fun—a pleasure to step into, fine to step out in!

Biggest surprise is the Ranchero's modest price. See for yourself how the Ranchero combines sleeves-up spunk with coats-on style. See it at your Ford Dealers!

For '57—and the years ahead

FORD TRUCKS COST LESS
...LESS TO OWN...LESS TO RUN...LAST LONGER, TOO!

1957
RANCHERO

Ford pioneered the car-pickup concept with the 1957 Ranchero, which debuted alongside the Skyliner retractable hardtop on December 8, 1956, at the New York Auto Show. The Ranchero was a clever spin-off of Ford's two-door Ranch Wagon, and many components interchanged between the two models. The Ranchero's six-foot-long pickup bed offered 32.4 square feet of cargo space, which was more than some standard pickup beds of the day. The examples pictured here are uplevel Custom versions—base Rancheros had no chrome sidespear and could not be ordered with the optional two-tone paint. Buyers must have preferred the extra flash, as Customs outsold the base models 15,277 to 6429.

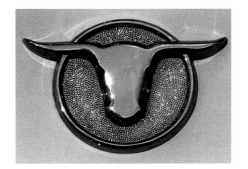

Ford's rugged body defied the world's toughest roads. The ancient roads of Asia proved the hard way that the 58 Ford's new body stays quiet and tight. Here's a car that's really *proven* that it's built for keeps.

Ford's fine-car coachwork impressed English craftsmen. Skillful, fine-car body work...new, carefully tailored fittings...doors that close solid as a bank vault. Here, indeed, is truly royal company for a royal coach.

Best in build around the world

Best for savings, too!

You save when you buy, *and* in the long run! Ford's round-the-world test *proved* Ford bodies are built better. Why not? *Five* braces provide superior strength in the new Slipstream roof—compared with three or less in competitive cars. Under those graceful body contours is the most insulation in Ford's field. Ford's exclusive wide-base frame and superior body mounting provide lasting rigidity, quieter ride, greater safety. You can't buy better in *build!*

Smart New York shoppers agreed: you can't buy better! Visit your Ford Dealer soon to Action Test the all-new 58 Ford and check its low, low price!

58 FORD

Proved and approved around the world

1958
FAIRLANE 500

Fords received a fairly heavy-handed facelift for 1958, which included quad headlights and taillights, a bulky front bumper/grille, dummy hood scoop, and new bodyside trim. Ford bragged that its '58 cars were "proved and approved around the world" in globe-hopping road tests. The '58s also boasted Ford's first three-speed automatic transmission and a pair of all-new big-block V-8s. The 332-cid version made 240 horsepower with a two-barrel carburetor and a single exhaust, or 265 hp with a four-barrel and duals. The performance-oriented 352-cid "Thunderbird Interceptor Special" made 300 hp with a four-barrel, dual exhaust, and 10.2:1 compression. The Fairlane 500 Victoria hardtop coupe (right) accounted for 80,439 sales.

67

NEW FORD **THUNDERBIRD**

The most wanted, most admired car in America
— and it's priced <u>far</u> below other luxury cars!

The new Thunderbird convertible decisively proves
that you *can* have your cake and eat it, too.

For now you can have true Thunderbird performance and Thunderbird fun—and, at the same time,
luxurious room and comfort for *four* lucky people.

Your T-bird comes equipped for superior performance with the brilliant new 300-hp Thunderbird Special
V-8. Imagine what this beautiful new power plant
means in a car so low, so lithe, so compact!

When the hide-away top is down, the rear deck is
perfectly *flush* with the rear seats, forming one
smooth, uninterrupted line of Thunderbird beauty.

See America's most individual car at your Ford
Dealer's soon. You've nothing to lose but your heart!

ANOTHER FIRST FROM FORD

Completely new Thunderbird hardtop trunk gives you
20 cubic feet of space. You can take four big suitcases, golf
bags, other gear. And Thunderbird's wide, wide doors give
direct, easy access to all four luxuriously comfortable seats!

Every Ford has SAFETY GLASS in every window

1958
THUNDERBIRD

A new breed of Thunderbird debuted for 1958,
with seating for four instead of two. Purists
moaned, but sales shot up to 37,892, nearly
doubling 1957 output. Of those, just 2134 were
convertibles; due to construction delays, ragtops
didn't reach showrooms until the summer of '58.
The new models gained the nickname "squarebird"
for their blocky shape. Styling highlights included a
gaping mesh-filled bumper/grille, quad headlamps
beneath "gullwing" hoods, prominent upper body-
side creaseline and lower sculptured "bomb," and
a broad deck ending in two wide rectangles, each
holding a pair of large round taillamps. The sole
engine choice was Ford's new FE-series 352 V-8,
which put out 300 horsepower.

Married in style and luxury! The 59 Thunderbird and the new Ford Galaxie

ANNOUNCING — THE NEW FORD *Galaxie*

Brilliant wedding of Thunderbird elegance and the world's most beautifully proportioned cars

The 59 Fords awarded the Gold Medal of the Comite Francais de L'Elegance for beautiful proportions at the Brussels World's Fair.

Just married in style to the Thunderbird! It's the smartest, richest and most exciting of 59 Fords—the elegant new Galaxie. A bright new personality in cars—and more! The Galaxie is a full "fine car" 6-passenger expression of Thunderbird grace—spirit—style and luxury in an altogether-new line of Fords.

It's Thunderbird in looks! The Galaxie, as you'll quickly see, is as wonderfully all-the-way Thunderbird as a low-priced Ford can be. The smart straight-line

Galaxie roof and dramatic see-it-all rear window say Thunderbird *unmistakably*. So do the clean, crisp, low-swept body lines. Here is the most perfect match yet of the Thunderbird's silhouette—the most modern and most wanted "new look" in cars today!

It's Thunderbird in luxury! New Galaxie appointments—like the plush, deep-pile carpets—are so very Thunderbird in taste. And just like the Thunderbird, the Galaxie seats you in the tailored elegance of specially

quilted and pleated fabrics. There's Thunderbird V-8 power, too. A surpassing luxury that tells you how superbly these newlyweds "GO" together.

Reception now—you are invited. Why not come in —this very week—see the new Galaxie and all the members of the year's most beautiful wedding. The experience, we bet, will please you proud. It might even set you to planning a second honeymoon—most elegantly—in the car that's Thunderbird in everything *except price!*

Reception starting this week at your Ford Dealer's

70

1959
GALAXIE

Fords were totally restyled for 1959, wearing new body panels and revised inner structure on the 1957–58 chassis. Up front, hooded quad headlamps sat above a full-width grille and four rows of floating "stars." In the rear, a "Flying V" back panel was fixed over large round taillights in ribbed "Iris Eyes" reflectors. The luxurious Galaxie line debuted at midyear, bumping the Fairlane 500 from its perch at the top of the Ford model roster. Galaxie advertising focused heavily on the line's similarities to the popular T-Bird, boasting of "Thunderbird Elegance." Galaxie Town Sedans, like this Geranium and Colonial White example, started at $2582. They were the most popular members of the Galaxie lineup, with sales of 183,108.

the long, sophisticated line

that flows

through Ford

styling

has become

the
silver
curve of
success

The long, elegant silver curve now moving over the American Road on hundreds of thousands of 1960 Fords has become the hallmark of success. To its last beautifully proportioned inch, this is the decisive style of the decade, a direction-pointer as certain as a compass needle.

The Galaxie is a clear-cut expression of the newest Ford styling trend — the uniquely formal roof balancing beautifully on the graceful sweep of its long, sophisticated body. Here, in Ford, you find distinctive automotive luxury at its finest . . . the first fashion of the sixties in America's best-selling car — the car with the *silver curve of success*.

Galaxie
by Ford

1960
GALAXIE

Ford redesigned its mainstream passenger cars for 1960 with the cleanest styling in years. Glass area was greatly increased, and the expected longer-lower-wider dimensions made for very spacious interiors. The new look was a marked deviation from previous Ford design themes, which didn't sit well with some shoppers. Horizontal tailfins looked snazzy but made for an impractically narrow trunk opening. Pictured here are the Galaxie Town Sedan and Sunliner convertible, which started at $2603 and $2860, respectively. Optional equipment included power windows ($102), full-disc wheel covers ($17), seat belts ($21), and Polar-Aire air conditioning ($404 with V-8 and tinted glass).

See "FORD STARTIME" in living color Tuesdays on NBC   Ford Falcon: easiest car in the world to own

Introducing a wonderful new world of savings
in the new-size 1960 Ford *Falcon*

Look at the price tag for big news! For all its big-car comfort, styling and power, the Falcon delivers *for less* than many imported economy cars.

Honest-to-goodness six-passenger comfort. Plenty of room for six . . . and all their luggage!

New 6-cylinder engine . . . up front for greater safety and stability. A brand-new power plant specifically designed to power the Falcon over America's hills and highways with "big car" performance and safety.

World's most experienced new car. The Falcon was proven over every mile of numbered Federal Highway in Experience Run, U.S.A., a grueling demon-

stration climaxing Ford's 3 years and 3 million miles of testing and development.

Up to 30 miles a gallon on regular gas. Experience Run, U.S.A., proved the Falcon's exceptional gas mileage and oil economy.

Made in U.S.A. . . . . serviced everywhere. The Falcon is a product of Dearborn, Michigan, automotive capital of the world. Every part of the Falcon has been designed for maximum durability and dependable performance. Falcon service is available at over 7,000 Ford Dealers across the country.

FORD DIVISION, *Ford Motor Company,*

FORD BUILDS THE WORLD'S MOST BEAUTIFULLY PROPORTIONED CARS

 FORD—The Finest Fords of a Lifetime FALCON—The New-Size Ford   THUNDERBIRD—The World's Most Wanted Car

1960
FALCON

Ford entered the blossoming compact car market in 1960 and scored a home run. Falcon rang up nearly 436,000 sales to trump Chevrolet's rear-engined Corvair and Chrysler's odd-looking Valiant, competitors that also debuted for 1960. The Falcon was just 70.3 inches wide and weighed in at around 2300–2500 pounds—nearly a foot narrower and more than 1000 pounds lighter than the average full-size Ford. An all-new 144-cid inline six was the sole engine. It delivered 90 horsepower and fuel economy figures in the 25–30 mpg range. Base prices were penny-pinching as well; two-door sedans started at $1912, while four-door sedans cost $62 more. Rounding out the Falcon lineup were two- and four-door wagons and the newly downsized Ranchero.

Announcing...the 1961 Ford
beautifully proportioned to the **CLASSIC FORD LOOK**

Here is the eternally beautiful Galaxie Club Victoria in Rome's famous Piazza del Campidoglio.

BEAUTIFULLY BUILT TO TAKE CARE OF ITSELF

Ford makes automotive history with the trend-setting car of our times...a car that goes 30,000 miles without lubrication...4,000 miles between oil changes ...adjusts its own brakes...and is beautifully built to take care of you!

The 1961 Ford, already recognized for its beautiful proportions by a leading international fashion authority, introduces a whole new concept of what a car can do for you ... *and for itself!*

It lubricates itself. New nylon bearings and a newly developed lubricant keep the '61 Ford freshly greased for 30,000 miles. Good-bye, grease racks!

It cleans its own oil. The 1961 Ford's wonderfully efficient full-flow oil filtering system lets you go 4,000 miles between oil changes.

It adjusts its own brakes. A "mechanical brain" keeps brakes adjusted for the life of the lining.

Rust? Ford's body is specially processed to resist corrosion, even to galvanizing the body panels beneath

the doors. The bright metal trim has all been treated in depth to gleam and *stay* gleaming.

Ford takes care of itself on the turnpike, too. A new 390 cu. in. Thunderbird Special V-8 has all the punch you'll ever need. Two additional V-8's and a great Mileage Maker Six all thrive on regular gas.

Best of all, the '61 Ford is beautifully built to take care of you. No windshield dogleg nips your knees. Doors are extra wide for easy entry.

This is the 1961 Ford ... beautifully proportioned to the Classic Ford Look ... beautifully built to take care of itself.

HERE'S HOW THE '61 FORD TAKES CARE OF ITSELF

Lubricates itself. You'll normally go 30,000 miles without a chassis lubrication.

Cleans its own oil. You'll go 4,000 miles between oil changes with Ford's Full-Flow oil filter.

Adjusts its own brakes. New truck-size brakes adjust themselves automatically.

Guards its own muffler. Ford mufflers are double-

wrapped and aluminized—normally will last three times as long as ordinary mufflers.

Protects its own body. All vital underbody parts are specially processed to resist rust and corrosion, even to galvanizing body panels beneath doors.

Takes care of its own finish. New Diamond Lustre Finish never needs wax.

FORD DIVISION *Ford Motor Company.*

An honor to be proud of, this is the medal presented by the international fashion authority, Centro per l'Alta Moda Italiana, to the 1961 Ford for functional expression of *classic beauty.*

'61 FORD

1961
GALAXIE

A deft lower-body reskin gave full-size 1961 Fords a simple, pleasing new look. A clean new concave grille used a horizontal bar ahead of a "polka-dot" background whose texture was simply stamped in rather than composed of multiple buttons. Large round taillamps returned after a year's absence, topped by tiny fins recalling 1957 styling. A T-Bird-style squared-off roofline again capped line-topping Galaxie models like this $2664 Town Victoria four-door hardtop. Expanding big-Ford engine options was a new 390-cid V-8 offering 300 horsepower standard, with 330, 375, and a mighty 401 hp available. Nineteen sixty-one was the first full year that Lee Iacocca headed the Ford division—Robert McNamara had left in mid-1960 to become U.S. Secretary of Defense.

for the man who thought he had everything!

GALAXIE 500/XL. This one defines "luxury" better than a dictionary. It has all-new interior trim . . . foam-cushioned bucket seats separated by a Thunderbird-style console . . . and a 4-speed stick shift or automatic transmission. With a 405-hp Thunderbird V-8 engine, it'll outperform America's most expensive cars. As for service, the XL needs it only twice a year, or every 6,000 miles. This lively blend of elegance and action is now appearing in person at your Ford Dealer's. The line forms to the right!

A PRODUCT OF
Ford
MOTOR COMPANY

Galaxie 500/XL

Live it up with a Lively One from FORD

FALCON FAIRLANE GALAXIE THUNDERBIRD

1962
GALAXIE 500

Another lower-body reskin gave full-size Fords a squarer look for 1962. A flatter grille replaced the concave design of '61, and the gold "star" that had resided on Ford rooflines the previous two years migrated to the center of the grille. Out back, tailfins disappeared, and the taillights were set into scooped recesses in the bumper. Galaxie now denoted the most affordable sedans; a new upscale "Galaxie 500" line also listed hardtops and this Sunliner convertible. A bucket-seat hardtop and Sunliner arrived at midseason under "The Lively Ones" banner. Early in the model year, Ford unleashed its first 400-plus-cid engine: the burly 406 V-8. It made 395 horsepower with a four-barrel carburetor, or 405 hp with triple two-barrels.

Just right – for just about everybody!

There's no new car anything like it! A foot shorter than the big ones, the new Ford Fairlane 500 fits in your garage as prettily as it sits on a beach. Its bigness is *inside*—where it's as roomy as some of the biggest Fords ever built. Although priced under many compacts, the new Fairlane 500 is a fine car from dual headlights to oversize trunk. The all-new Challenger V-8 engine (optional) is the world's first Economy Eight—and is as quick to save a dollar as it is to save time. Service has been reduced to a minimum—30,000 miles on many items, no more than twice a year or 6,000 miles on the rest . . . A dream car? It was until this year. Now you can see it and drive it at your Ford Dealer's.

'62 FORD *FAIRLANE 500*
ONLY THE NAME'S THE SAME!

1962
FAIRLANE 500

Built to fit in between the ever-enlarging standard-size cars of the early Sixties and the then-new domestic compacts, the Ford Fairlane appeared to be a fresh type of car when it debuted in 1962. Essentially an enlarged Falcon riding a 115.5-inch wheelbase, Fairlane bowed with two- and four-door sedans in plain and fancy 500 trim, plus a bucket-seat 500 two-door. Falcon's larger six was standard, but two new "Challenger" V-8s were available: a 145-hp 221 and a lively 164-hp 260. New car buyers heartily approved, and Fairlane got off to a strong start with more than 297,000 sales. Fairlane 500 four-door sedans started at $2304— options such as power steering and brakes, back up lights, and the 221 V-8 pushed the price of this Sandshell Beige example to $2537.

for 1962 four new Thunderbirds

Today the car that brings the boldest new ideas to the American road is multiplied four times. For now there are *four* new Thunderbird models . . . paced by a unique expression of total luxury, the limited-edition Sports Roadster.

Sleek as a racing hydroplane, arrogantly individual in its gleaming sweep of deck, this is the most exciting invitation to two-passenger travel ever issued . . . but removal of the tonneau cover reveals the standard Thunderbird rear seat when four must journey. (Particularly pleasant is the fact that the top can be raised with the tonneau cover in place.) There's also a Thunderbird in evening dress, the Landau coupe with leather-grained vinyl top; plus new versions of the four-passenger Hardtop and the swift-lined Convertible.

All four pure Thunderbird, all sparkling with original Thunderbird ideas, from Swing-Away Steering Wheel to "floating" rear view mirror . . . and all crafted to Thunderbird standards of extraordinary quality. See them at your Ford Dealer's.

Thunderbird Sports Roadster—The slip-stream headrests are an integral part of the Sports Roadster's distinctive lift-off tonneau cover. Standard equipment includes full-chrome wire wheels and a passenger assist bar, plus the Swing-Away Steering Wheel found on all Thunderbirds.

The padded, leather-grained vinyl top of the Landau coupe expresses the Thunderbird spirit in terms of formal elegance, adds a traditional accent in the landau S-bar.

The sleek prow of the Hardtop sheathes the secret of Thunderbird's torrential power—the 390 Special V-8 with four-barrel carburetion.

The Convertible conceals its top, automatically, at the flick of a switch. There's no cloth boot to attach, no bulge to break the flawless sweep of line.

1962
THUNDERBIRD

After a complete redesign for 1961, the Thunderbird saw trim and detail changes for '62. The sleek, fuselage-like shape and pointed prow of the 1961–63 T-Birds earned them the "Bulletbird" nickname. Answering pleas for another two-seat T-Bird was the new-for-'62 Sports Roadster, basically the regular ragtop with a removable fiberglass tonneau hiding the rear seat. The forward end of the integral headrests mated with the tops of the front seats. The $5439 Sports Roadster cost $651 more than a regular convertible and sold just 1427 copies. Attractive Kelsey-Hayes wire wheels came standard on the Sports Roadster, but not the rear fender skirts seen here.

Ford presents the Liveliest of the Lively Ones!

The new Command Performance cars—fresh from their world premiere in the Principality of Monaco

Overlooking Monaco: 63½ Super Torque Ford Sports Hardtop, 63½ Falcon Sprint, 63½ Fairlane Sports Coupe

Turn page ▶

1963
GALAXIE 500XL

Ford introduced a handful of sporty special edition cars as "1963 ½" models. The lineup included the Falcon Sprint two-door hardtop, a Fairlane 500 Sport Coupe two-door hardtop with a racy new 289-cid V-8, and a Galaxie 500 Sports Hardtop with an aerodynamic "slantback" roof. The new roofline's slicker aerodynamics were a big plus in long-distance stock-car races, combining with competition-tuned big-block V-8s to make Ford the season champ in NASCAR. This "slantback" 500 XL packs the gutsy triple-carb, 405-horsepower 406, but Ford rolled out an even stronger engine as a midyear option: the dual-quad, 425-hp 427. The Ford "Total Performance" era was nigh.

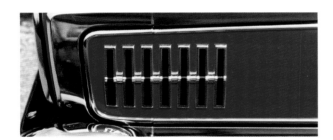

FORD GALAXIE 500 2-DOOR HARDTOP

"3½-speed" box–and no charge

Every standard-shift Ford has Synchro on Low gear. Same for V-8 version of Fairlane and Falcon. That takes the old three-speeder out of Dullsville; making the bottom cog a *driving* gear instead of just a start-up gear is like adding half a ratio to the box and even the most basic Ford you can buy gets a good chunk of that sports car feeling.

How do you explain this to mama, who thinks Synchro is a new detergent?

Well, you can take her out in a '64 Ford and say: "Look, here I am almost stopped and the light goes green–so I pop it into Low and away we go; no "crr-r-runch." Or you can show her the bit about the slow truck and the short

straightaway–how you can flip into Low at 10 M.P.H. and squirt on by with a big safety margin. Or sail down a stiff mountain grade and get the braking assist of bottom gear any time you want it. Or shift in the middle of a climbing hairpin turn without losing momentum.

We feel Synchro Low adds a big chunk of pleasure to anybody's three-speed driving. That's a big chunk you don't get in any other standard-shift car–because only Ford takes the trouble.

So trot on down to your Ford dealer and try it; we may wean you away from automatics yet.

1964
GALAXIE 500XL

Ford designers went all-out to make their '64 full-sizers look fresh and new, resulting in the most thorough and dramatic year-to-year styling change since 1960. The effort paid off—sales of full-size Fords topped the 900,000 mark for the year (their best sales performance for the 1962–64 period) and Motor Trend awarded its "Car of the Year" honor to the year's entire Ford line. The crisp new body lines looked especially striking in two-door hardtop form, as this top-line Galaxie 500 XL demonstrates. Space-saving "thin-shell" front bucket seats were a new feature seen on Galaxie 500 XLs and redesigned T-Birds. The big-Ford dash was slightly modified from '63, but XL interior trim was as brightly lavish as ever.

Ford Motor Company is:

a finishing school

Our lesson for today is paint.

The word to remember is *acrylic*—the name of a brilliant new enamel finish pioneered on cars by Ford Motor Company.

Acrylic enamels are 50% harder—which means an extra bright original luster and greater resist-ance to sun, salt, stones, scuffs and scratches.

They also retain their brilliance longer, even without waxing.

Acrylic enamels are glowing evidence that—when it comes to quality—a Ford Motor Com-pany car outshines anything in its class.

Ford-built means better built MUSTANG · FALCON · FAIRLANE · FORD
COMET · MERCURY
THUNDERBIRD · LINCOLN CONTINENTAL

1965
GALAXIE 500XL

Full-size Fords were virtually clean-sheet new for
1965, with taut, chiseled styling and new-design
frame with wider tracks, revised suspension, and
side-rail "torque boxes" that damped out noise
and harshness. Ford's ad writers were quick to
promote the new lineup's hushed performance;
a provocative ad campaign claimed "Ford rides
quieter than Rolls-Royce." With Chrysler's tempo-
rary withdrawal from NASCAR racing, Fords had
a banner year on the stock-car circuit, winning 48
of 55 events. A plush LTD coupe and sedan were
the new flagship models of the Galaxie 500 series,
but the sportiest big Ford hardtop was the Galaxie
500XL coupe, priced this year from $3233. A little
more than 28,000 were built.

The Private World of Thunderbird for 1965

This is Thunderbird for 1965. Unique. Thoughtful. Here, automotive trends are set. And, this year, Thunderbird is again the innovator. Start with the Sequential Taillight Turn Signal . . . three lights in each taillight that flash, in sequence, in the direction of your turn. It is Thunderbird's alone . . . and standard. In fact, there are many Thunderbird extras you don't pay extra for: front-wheel disc brakes, power steering, Swing-Away steering wheel, radio, Silent-Flo ventilation, retractable seat belts and more. Other fine touches: optional warning lights to tell you when a door is ajar, fuel is low. But, as always, the most exciting part of the Thunderbird adventure is the way the car moves and rides and corners. Other cars you drive . . . this one you Thunderbird. Discover Thunderbird's Private World for 1965 at your Ford Dealer's.

Thunderbird
Unique in all the world

1965
THUNDERBIRD

After their complete redesign for 1964, Thunderbirds wore only minor trim updates for 1965, including a new grille texture, T-Bird logo hood badge, and front-fender "C-spear" chrome trim. Front disc brakes were a welcome engineering improvement, given that T-Bird curb weights were in the 4500-pound range. A healthy 300-horsepower 390 V-8 carried on as the standard powerplant, but the emphasis was still on classy comfort first, performance second. The Thunderbird remained at the forefront of the burgeoning personal-luxury market, boasting such "with-it" features as wide taillights with three-segment sequential turn signals, lounge-like wraparound rear seats, and a swing-away steering column for easier driver-seat access.

1965
FAIRLANE

Fairlanes got a somewhat busier look for 1965, with knife-edge fenderlines and prominent body-side creases à la this year's redesigned full-size Fords. Wheelbase added a nominal half-inch to 116 even, but the basic design was still 1962 and had plenty of newer competition. These and other factors combined to push Fairlane model-year sales below 224,000, a new low for Ford's midsize line. The year's rarest Fairlane proved to be the base two-door sedan; just 13,685 were made. This Silversmoke grey example is unusually equipped with fender skirts, bumper guards, and the 200-horsepower 289 V-8 with three-speed overdrive transmission.

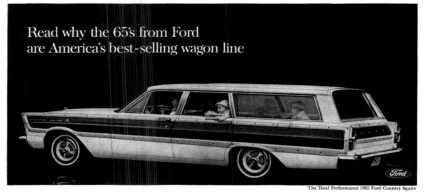

1965
FALCON SQUIRE

Ford's wagon lineup offered ritzy wood-look trim on both the full-size Country Squire and compact Falcon Squire models but not on the intermediate-size Fairlane wagon series. Falcon models saw only minor trim updates for 1965 after receiving a handsome lower-body reskin for '64. Standard Falcon powerplant was the 101-horsepower, 170-cubic-inch inline six, but another $153 bought a significantly peppier 289 V-8 with 200 hp. Overall Falcon production dropped significantly for '65 to 213,601, due to increased competition from rival automakers and Ford's own wildly popular Mustang. The original Falcon had finally run its course, and a totally re-engineered Falcon lineup would debut for 1966.

Mustang . . . a look that becomes you in cars and sunglasses

Renauld's wild new sunglasses, the Mustang, come in six lens colors. Choose from Green, Gray, Bronze, Blue, Pastel Gray and Champagne. And the frames give you a choice, too—shades that mix or match the colors of Ford's great new road car!

*Mustang
is designed
to be designed
by you!*

Mustang invites creativity in its owner—it's the car designed to be designed by you. By dipping into a surprisingly wide array of options, you can make your Mustang as personal as your signature.

Make your trips to school or the super-market a lot more fun by choosing such convenience options as: power steering and brakes, Cruise-O-Matic transmission, push-button radio, backup lights, whitewall tires, deluxe seat belts for those in the back as well as the front, and an outside rearview mirror for a better look at the road behind.

Or make your Mustang an all-out luxury car to suit your special taste for elegance: choose a vinyl-covered roof, an accent paint stripe, an air conditioner, padded sun visors, tinted glass, and a full-length console to hold your scarf and sunglasses.

And if you're looking for the ultimate in action—or if the man in your life is—tailor your Mustang into a true sports car. Just equip it with a 289-cu. in. V-8 engine, a 4-speed transmission, Rally Pac (tachometer and clock), and wire-style wheel covers.

For a scale model of the Mustang, send $1.00 to Mustang Offer, Dept. I, P.O. Box 35, Troy, Mich. (Offer ends July 31, 1964)

**TRY TOTAL PERFORMANCE
FOR A CHANGE!**

FORD

Mustang · Falcon · Fairlane · Ford · Thunderbird

RIDE WALT DISNEY'S MAGIC SKYWAY AT THE FORD MOTOR COMPANY'S WONDER ROTUNDA, NEW YORK WORLD'S FAIR

1965
MUSTANG

Ford's landmark Mustang was an early 1965 debut, though many enthusiasts—and sometimes Ford itself—use "1964 ½" to describe early build models. For the "formal" 1965 season, Mustang got several changes, including a larger base six and three optional 289 V-8s instead of a single 260. The convertible at right carries the optional GT package, which delivered such goodies as fog lamps, lower-bodyside stripes, firmer suspension, and extra gauges. Power front-disc brakes arrived as a separate late-season extra priced at just $58. Mustang ragtop sales tallied nearly 102,000 in the ponycar's extra-long debut model year, compared to nearly 502,000 hardtop coupe models. Clearly, Ford had a bona-fide hit on its hands.

Villarceaux, built in 1755, is a jewel of French château architecture, is packed with period treasures in furniture, tapestries, paintings. The cars: a 1966 Ford XL and a hand-fitted Citroen Chapron, made by the greatest custom coachbuilder in France.

Ford's Quiet Man reports from France:

"I was sure the Citroen Chapron would be quieter, because it is hand-made," said Count de Villefranche... but the new Ford XL quickly changed his opinion!

The Quiet Man demonstrates Ford's new Stereo Tape System with a snap-in cartridge that plays more than 70 minutes of continuous music.

Count Emmanuel de Villefranche was amused when the Quiet Man, touring Europe, challenged him to test the extraordinary hush of Ford's 1966 XL . . .

but he was intrigued. The French nobleman has two chateaux on his 2000-acre estate, a town house in Paris, a villa in Rome . . . and a polished appreciation for everything that is excellent.

He met the Quiet Man at the gates of Chateau Villarceaux with the most exclusive car made in France today, a handcrafted Citroen Chapron "Majestic." The "springs" of this car are spheres of nitrogen, compressed by oil. The body is all leather-lined, even the roof, and every part is fitted by hand by Henri Chapron's 170 craftsmen.

It is a very quiet car. But when Count de Villefranche finished driving the Ford XL he said: "It seems to me most remarkable a factory-made car like this could be more quiet, more grand

luxe than a car made individually by the craftsmen."

The Quiet Man agreed that it is remarkable . . . but not when you consider the tremendous resources of Ford engineering, the great strength of the body, the refinements like "recessive" front wheels that flex *horizontally* a trifle to take the thump out of bumps.

Count de Villefranche was fascinated by the Ford, particularly by the new Stereo Tape System and its 70-minute snap-in tape cartridges. He exclaimed: "What wonderful sound . . . it is like the whole orchestra was in the auto!" You will be fascinated too, when you drive an XL like the one Count de Villefranche tested. Your Ford dealer has one waiting.

AMERICA'S TOTAL PERFORMANCE CARS

FORD

1966
GALAXIE 500

Full-size Fords were updated for 1966 with slightly curvier contours. Advertising aimed for an air of international sophistication and continued to promote the big Fords' quietness; this ad pits a Galaxie 500XL two-door hardtop against the hand-built Citroen Chapron. Topping the Galaxie 500 lineup was the 7-Litre, which came as a $3872 ragtop or a $3621 hardtop coupe. Named for the metric size of Ford's new 428-cid FE-series V-8 (345 horsepower, or 360 hp in Police Interceptor tune), these cruisers did 0–60 mph in 8 seconds. Galaxie 500XL and 7-Litre models shared handsome bucket seat interiors that were trimmed generously with chrome and woodgrain.

1966
FAIRLANE 500

Ford's midsize Fairlane was overhauled for 1966 with smooth new styling on wider bodies that left room for big-block V-8s. Among those bodies was a first-time convertible, offered along with hardtop coupes in 500/XL trim and new XL/GT guise. GTs were quick, thanks to a standard 335-horsepower 390 V-8. For those who wanted to go much faster, Ford also produced a small run of dragstrip-ready Fairlane hardtops equipped with the fire-breathing 425-horsepower 427 V-8 and a lift-off fiberglass hood with functional scoop. With 75,947 built, the Fairlane 500 hardtop was the most popular model in the lineup. Note the dealer-installed air conditioner in this 289-powered Emberglo example.

RANCHERO! All-new luxury!

Even standing still this beauty looks exciting. And no wonder. Those sleek lines cover a high-spirited Ranchero that's new clear through. A longer wheelbase, wider tread and new suspension give you a ride that's wonderfully smooth, soft and quiet.

Inside, curved side windows, greater shoulder width and swept-away dash give a luxurious new feeling of roominess. Bucket seats, center console, wall-to-wall carpeting, air-conditioning—Ranchero offers them all. Any performance combination you want, too—choice of a smooth Six or two powerful V-8's. Automatic, 3- or no-clash 4-speed stick shift.

Price? That's the only thing about the new Ford Ranchero that isn't big and luxurious.

A PRODUCT OF
Ford

1966
FALCON RANCHERO

Falcons were all-new for 1966, sporting a redesign that returned the line to its roots as a basic, affordable compact. Bodystyle offerings were pared down to a two-door coupe, four-door sedan, four-door wagon, and, for 1966 only, a Ranchero pickup. Ranchero buyers could choose from the $2330 standard model (right) or a better-equipped $2411 Deluxe (left). Base engine was a 120-horsepower, 200 cubic-inch six, but two 289 V-8s were optional—a two-barrel carb version with 200 hp, and a four-barrel carb version with 225. Ranchero sales had never been high, but this year's total was respectable at 21,760. For 1967, the Ranchero model would migrate to Ford's midsize Fairlane platform.

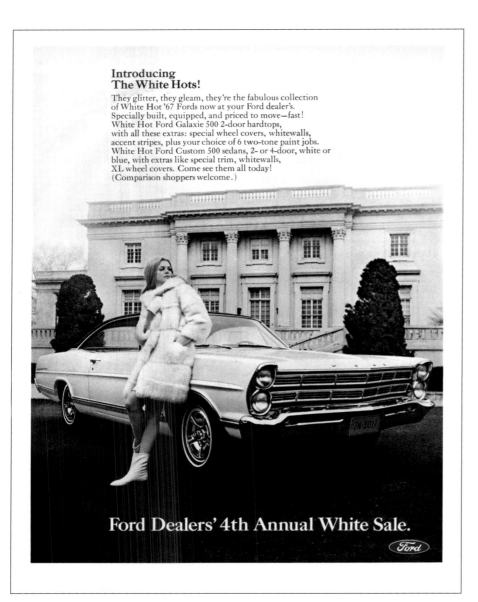

1967
GALAXIE 500

Full-size 1967 Fords kept their existing wheelbases but adopted more-flowing lines that added three inches to overall length. Hardtop coupes gained a smoother roofline, too. This Galaxie 500 version, which priced from $2755, repeated as the line's most popular single model by drawing 197,388 sales. In other big Ford news, LTD became a separate series and added a four-door sedan, while the big-block 7-Litre models became a package option for XLs. Galaxie 500s came standard with a 240-cid six, but the line also offered 289, 390, 427, and 428 V-8s. Dearborn marked another milestone in May 1967 with production of the 70-millionth car since the company's founding in 1903.

SHOW YOUR STRIPES!

That GT feeling is contagious: every Fairlane has it.

And every Fairlane owner knows it. The feeling that comes with driving a car that was built to perform. And gives you the luxury you've always wanted. Like Stereo Tape. Engines up to 427 cu. in. Air Conditioning. Show your stripes! Pick your Fairlane sedan, hardtop, convertible, or wagon – soon! **FAIRLANE**

1967
FAIRLANE 500XL

Fairlanes got minor trim updates for 1967. This year, Fairlane GTs formed a separate series with the slightly less sporty 500XL hardtop and convertible. XLs saw respective sales of 14,871 and just 1943. In another change, GTs were demoted to a 200-horsepower 289 V-8. Big-block 390s now cost extra and delivered 270 or 320 hp. GTs priced from $2839 for the hardtop, $3064 for the soft top. Garden-variety Fairlane GTs were outmuscled on the street by rival GTOs, GTXs, and Chevelle SS 396s, but 427-powered Fairlanes held their own in dragstrip competition. On the NASCAR circuit, Mario Andretti scored his only Daytona 500 victory in a 427-powered Fairlane this year.

1967
MUSTANG

The 1967 Mustangs got a full outer-body reskin that made for a huskier look and added two inches to overall length. Coupes, ragtops, and fastbacks were back with a new nose and concave tail panel. Wider engine bays had space for the new 320-horsepower 390 big-block V-8, while the 200-cid six and 289 V-8s were carried over. Ford finally faced direct competition for '67 in a much-revised Plymouth Barracuda and Chevrolet's new Camaro. Overall, Mustang sales fell 23 percent, but Ford still sold 474,121 for the model year, making it by far the No. 1 ponycar. The 289-powered Night Mist Blue fastback shown at right is one of just 200 or so "T-5" export models.

QUIET. STRONG. BEAUTIFUL.

A GREAT ROAD CAR.

'68 FORD.

How do you build a great road car? You start with a good car and keep making it better. In 1965 Ford built a good car—an LTD so good it rode quieter than a Rolls-Royce. In 1966 a Ford showed itself quieter than many of Europe's most expensive cars. And in 1967 a Ford was strong enough to hurtle eight punishing steeplechase jumps...and stay quiet. They were good Fords. Good and quiet. Good and strong. Today's Ford? It's just a little better than last year's. That's what makes it great.

FACTS ABOUT THE '68 FORD LTD: Most luxurious of the 21 new Fords for '68. 3 models available, 4-door sedan, 4-door hardtop, and 2-door hardtop. Better ideas include the new 302-cu. in. V-8, disappearing headlamps, wood-like paneling on doors and instrument panel, all standard. Options like improved SelectShift transmission (3 forward speeds, works both manually and automatically). V-8's up to 428-cu. in., including a 390-cu. in. V-8 that runs on regular gas. Power front disc brakes as the regular brake option. All push-button AM/FM Stereo Radio. SelectAire Conditioner. More.

See the light!

FORD

Ford has a better idea

1968
XL

All 1968 big Fords wore new, more-formal lower-body sheetmetal and reverted from vertical to horizontal headlamps. Luxurious LTDs and sporty XLs shared a handsome hidden-headlamp face. The LTD hardtop coupe (left) wore a formal roofline. The XL coupe (right) boasted a rakish, fastback-style "SportsRoof" that looked great but compromised rear visibility and usable trunk space. This example wears accessory exhaust tips and spotlights. Side marker lights were a new government requirement for '68—the front units were cleverly intergrated into the parking lights on big Fords. The long-running "Ford has a better idea" ad slogan debuted this year.

Sidney spent Sundays seashelling at the seashore. Then Sidney started digging the '68 Mustang—the great original. Dug the models: hardtop, fastback and convertible. Liked the low price, too, which left Sidney lots of clams to design his own Mustang, Sidney style. Now Sidney's making waves all over. Last week he saved 3 bathing beauties. (And they all could swim better than Sidney!)

Only Mustang makes it happen!

Mustang Fastback GT

FACTS ABOUT THE 1968 MUSTANG: Mustang's list of standard equipment can't be matched by any other sporty car in its price range. Includes floor-mounted stick shift with fully synchronized 3-speed transmission, bucket seats, door-to-door carpeting, all-vinyl trim, 5-pod instrument cluster. And Mustang gives you a range of options no competitor offers. Like SelectShift with 3 forward speeds—can be used as a manual or an automatic; available with any model, any engine. Or an all-pushbutton AM Radio/Stereosonic Tape System. V-8's up to 390 cu. in. And the broadest choice of performance options around: including a special heavy-duty suspension, front power disc brakes on all models, wide-oval tires, and more.

FORD
has a better idea

1968
MUSTANG

Mustangs got trim detail changes for 1968, among them a new grille insert with "floating" running-horse emblem, revised side scoops, and federally mandated side-marker lights. GT models wore new styled steel wheels with GT hubcaps, and, for an extra charge, distinctive "C-stripe" bodyside graphics. A serious muscle upgrade came at midseason with the introduction of the 428 Cobra Jet engine, which made Mustangs a true dragstrip threat. Hardtop output hit 249,447 for the model year, while the handsome fastback saw sales of 42,581. Overall, Mustang sales dipped about 32 percent this year as the ponycar market matured and competitive models gained traction.

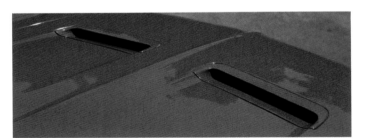

3-DOOR AND 5-DOOR BIRDS FOR 1969

Now there's a sliding sunroof door available for 2- and 4-door Birds. (Touch a button and you see the moon and the stars!) And that's only part of the Bird's new flight gear for this year. There's standard equipment like a soaring 429 Thunderjet V-8 to expedite your take-off. And a full-width front seat that sets a new standard for comfort and luxury. And, of course, a skyful of options. Fly Thunderbird 1969. The view this year is high, wide and heavenly.

1969 Thunderbird 2-door Landau, with new optional sunroof door and bucket seats.

THUNDERBIRD *Ford*

1969
THUNDERBIRD

Thunderbirds wore cosmetic tweaks for 1969, after their clean-sheet redesign for 1967. A power-sliding steel sunroof, still a novelty on American cars, joined the options list. The T-Bird lineup offered two coupe models—the base hardtop (right) and the blind-quartered, vinyl-topped Landau (left)—and a Landau four-door sedan. The sole engine choice was a 360-horsepower "Thunder-jet" 429 V-8. Thunderbird production slumped to 49,272 this year—the lowest model-year tally since 1958. Increased competition from rival models, particularly the Buick Riviera and redesigned Pontiac Grand Prix, was one reason for the decline.

Ford Torino.
It came up the hard way, easy.

A pack of rough, tough supercars
is hard to beat. Specially
modified Torinos make it
look easy. Won all 3 U.S.
stock-car championships:
NASCAR, ARCA, USAC.
22 major trophies so far.

Easy to get excited about,
another nonstop winner:
Torino GT SportsRoof.
With new 428 Cobra Jet V-8
option. See Torino '69.
Moving out fast.

On tracks.
On highways.
Off showroom floors.

Cobra Jet **428**

For more information on 1969 Torino GT SportsRoof, write
Torino Catalog, Dept. 50, P. O. Box 1000, Dearborn, Mich. 48121.

TORINO *Ford*

116

1969

TORINO GT

Midsize Fords saw little change for 1969, after a complete 1968 redesign that also introduced the Torino nameplate. The Torino lineup stood upmarket from the Fairlane series and included sporty GT models such as the SportsRoof fastback coupe. Standard Torino GT engine was a 220-horsepower 302 V-8, but Ford's musclebound 428 Cobra Jet (conservatively rated at 335 hp) was optional. The Torino's wind-cheating fastback bodystyle made it a formidable competitor on the stock-car racing circuit, and Ford was happy to brag about it in advertising. Later in the model year, Ford introduced the droop-snoot Torino Talladega, which spurred Chrysler to counter with the slicked-up Dodge Charger 500 and outrageous Charger Daytona.

Survival of the fittest: Mustang is America's No.1 sporty car again.

1970
MUSTANG MACH I

The Mach 1 fastback coupe remained the hottest "volume" Mustang for 1970. Engine choices included the standard 250-horsepower, 351-cubic-inch V-8; a four-barrel 300-horse 351; or the potent 335-hp 428 Cobra Jet, with or without a ram air "shaker" hood scoop setup. All 1970 Mustangs wore a mild facelift that included recessed taillamps and a return to dual headlamps. Mach 1s wore unique ribbed lower-body trim, a special grille with driving lights, and hood/tail panel stripes. Mach 1s started at $3271, and sales hit a respectable 40,970. Mustang was indeed surviving, but overall output fell 50 percent for 1970, to a bit less than 191,000.

The answer
to low cost transportation
is simplicity itself.

Maverick, the original "simple machine," is answering a lot of questions...
    Fewer repair bills? Simple. According to an independent survey, Maverick has the lowest frequency-of-repair record of any American car.
    Better gas mileage? Simple. In simulated city/suburban driving, the standard 100-horsepower-six engine delivers an average of 22 miles per gallon. Less servicing? Simple. One-sixth as many lube jobs and one-half as many oil changes as the leading import. Easier parking? Simple. Maverick has the smallest turning circle of any U.S. compact. Longer life? Simple. Unitized body, deep-down rustproofing and four coats of electrostatically applied paint. And with Maverick, you can choose 2-door, 4-door or sporty Grabber model—with any of three sixes or V-8.
    Any more questions? See the simple machine at your Ford Dealer's.

MAVERICK
The Simple Machine

MAVERICK *Ford*

1970
MAVERICK

The penny-pinching Maverick was introduced midway through the 1969 model year as an early 1970 model. Advertising branded it "the first car of the '70s at 1960 prices," and with a starting price of $1995, it was hard to argue the claim. That money bought a very basic, mundane vehicle, but budget-minded shoppers didn't seem to mind: a whopping 578,914 Mavericks were produced during the long inaugural model year. For shoppers who craved a little more pizzazz, Ford introduced the Maverick Grabber package in spring 1970. It included a blackout grille and tail, tape graphics, fake air-scoop hood, "racing" mirrors, and 14-inch wheels with trim rings, but no true performance upgrades.

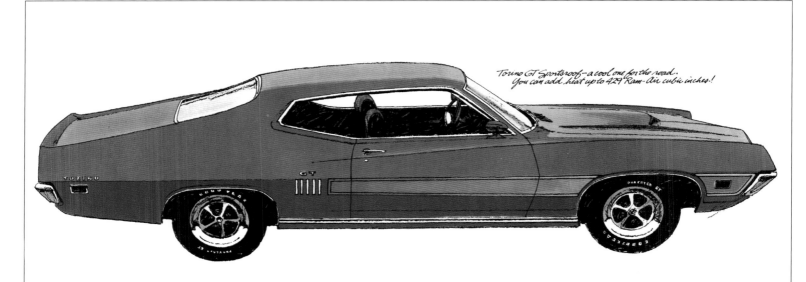

Torino GT Sportsroof—a cool one for the road.
You can add heat up to 429 Ram-Air cubic inches!

'70 Torino GT—beautiful way to go!

Torino GT Convertible.
The Pace Car for all America.

Torino GT is Cobra's luxury-lovin' cousin. But don't let all the glamour fool you. Under that new low silhouette you can choose your cubes—302, 351 or 429. Torino GT can be the kind of car you take to the strip Saturday afternoon, then use to make the scene Saturday night.

You can't lose for winning with the Torino GT because it's new—all new—from the inside out. It has to be the glamour-and-go car of 1970. Just take a look at what it has to offer in the go department . . . an optional Cobra Jet 429 Ram-Air with a through-the-hood Shaker. If that doesn't grab you, there are four—count them four—other V-8's! And remember with any of the 429 engines you get competition suspension that includes ultra heavy-duty springs, shocks and stabilizer bar. What about the glamour? Well, one reason why the GT looks so low and sneaky is that we made it over an inch lower and put a deeper slope—57 degrees—into the windshield. If you want to make it look about knee-high, order the new Laser Stripes. These are so wild some people think they should have a switch to turn them off. No doubt about it, when it came to styling we just couldn't stop ourselves. Black "egg-crate" grille, hidden wipers, wide-tread belted whitewalls, integral hood scoop, hidden taillamps, rear deck appliques, GT side badges, optional Hideaway Headlamps and argent styled steel wheels, but why go on . . . you get the idea. We built the year's best show-and-go machine.

These two pages tell you all about the 1970 Torino GT. They are part of Ford's 16-page '70 Performance Buyer's Digest. It includes detailed specifications and options on all the great 1970 performance Fords . . . Cobra, Torino GT, Boss 302, and Mach I. There are also sections on Ford performance fun vehicles and Ford Muscle Parts. The Digest wraps it all up for you. For a copy just write to:
FORD PERFORMANCE DIGEST, Dept. CL-1
Box 747, Dearborn, Michigan 48121

TORINO

1970
TORINO GT

Torinos got a swoopy redesign that netted Motor Trend's "Car of the Year" honors. Sporty GT models were the style leaders, boasting an optional hidden headlamp grille, non-functional hood scoop, full-width taillamp panel, and available "laser stripe" body-side graphics. A new-design 370- or 375-hp 429-cubic-inch V-8 replaced the 428 Cobra Jet as the top Torino performance-engine option. Torino GTs came only in SportsRoof hardtop coupe or convertible form, starting at $3105 and $3212, respectively. Just 3939 ragtops were produced, compared to 56,819 hardtops. Demand for drop-tops was slumping across the industry, and Ford would remove midsize convertibles from the lineup by 1972.

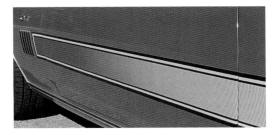

The Thunderbird Feeling:
Only when you drive one
can you truly experience it.

A great deal of that feeling comes from
what we call "The Thunderbird Ride."

The ride comes from Thunderbird's
new body/frame construction that
helps absorb road shock and vibration.
And a new suspension that's electron-
ically tuned to the steel-belted radial
tires for quiet, smooth road performance.

Another part of the feeling comes
from Thunderbird's luxurious interior
appointments—the enveloping comfort
of its seats, the lush, cut-pile carpeting
underfoot, and the increased roominess
made possible by a longer wheelbase.
They're all part of this magnificent
personal automobile.

But there's really only one sure
way to get the feeling of Thunderbird.
Drive it. At your Ford Dealer's now.

Options shown: glamour paint; vinyl roof; body side protection molding; power antenna; leather and vinyl individually adjustable seats.

THUNDERBIRD

FORD DIVISION · *Ford*

1972
THUNDERBIRD

The all-new Thunderbird now shared its basic
structure with the Lincoln Continental Mark IV and
was a much bigger 'Bird as a result. The standard
engine was a 429-cid V-8, but buyers could opt for
a 460-cube unit that generated 224 horsepower
under the newly accepted net power ratings. Ford
recorded a milestone in Thunderbird history when
the Gold Fire Metallic car at right—the 1-millionth
T-Bird—was produced in Los Angeles on June 22,
1972. It wore commemorative medallions in the
center of the decorative landau bars. At 57,814
units, T-Bird production was up by more than
21,000 cars from 1971, despite the fact that
there was only one body style from which to choose
instead of the previous three.

125

Control and balance make it a beautiful experience.

Most people look at waves and just see water. To them, a road's just pavement. But if you think there's more to life, we've got something for you.

Mustang's new Sprint Decor Option. Sporty colors inside and out. Dual racing mirrors that look right at home.

Even the interior of the Sprint Decor Option is a new experience. A panoramic instrument panel and a floor-mounted stick shift sitting between bucket seats. Now this is the real way to control a car.

Its stabilizer bar and independent front suspension help give you a more balanced ride. Around curves and over bumps.

The Sprint Decor Option is available in the Hardtop and SportsRoof models. Mag wheels, raised white letter tires and competition suspension are also available.

1972 Ford Mustang SportsRoof shown with Sprint Decor Option.

FORD MUSTANG

FORD DIVISION *Ford*

1972 Ford Mustang Hardtop shown with Sprint Decor Option.

1972
MUSTANG

Mustangs got larger, heavier, and more boldly styled in their 1971 redesign and saw only minor visual changes for '72. By the early 1970s, "spring specials" were a common manufacturer tactic to boost sales at the tail end of the model year. The Mustang's Sprint Decor Option, which debuted in March 1972, celebrated the '72 U.S. Olympic team. A basic "A" package included white paint with color-matched plastic-covered front bumper, broad blue body-accent stripes edged in red, racing mirrors, and bold "U.S.A." flag decals on the rear fenders. Interiors were color coordinated in vinyl with blue cloth inserts for the seats. A "B" package bundled all this with Magnum 500 wheels, F60-15 white-letter tires, and firm competition suspension.